Contents

Foreword

Excellence in assessing *is designed to help assessors develop their practice to the highest standards. QCA welcomes this addition, with its examples of good practice, to the assessors' toolkit.*

The quality of assessment has a major impact on the candidate being assessed, and the experience of assessment is a key factor in maintaining employer and public confidence in National Vocational Qualifications. For many adult learners, their managers and their employers, involvement with an assessor will be their only direct contact with the process of gaining an NVQ.

The Regulation and Standards Division of QCA is charged with regulating awarding bodies and their qualifications effectively so that the qualifications are fair, standards are secure, and public confidence is maintained. This means ensuring that candidates gaining an NVQ have a qualification that is fit for purpose and recognised by candidates and employers alike as having value in their industry.

Effectively and sensibly applied, the principles and suggestions contained within Excellence in assessing *will contribute to making the process of assessment a more effective method of recognising the achievements of learners.*

Isabel M. Nisbet

Isabel Nisbet
Director, Regulation and Standards
Qualifications and Curriculum Authority

Introduction

This guide is for assessors of NVQs and SVQs, and looks at the main methods of assessment and how to use them. The guide will help you carry out your duties as an assessor more efficiently, and give you the confidence to make the right assessment decisions and to stand by them.

The guide is for you if you are:

- *working towards the A1 Assessor Award (A1)*

- *qualified as an assessor under the old 'D' units, and keen to update your practice in line with the A1 standards*

- *assessing candidate assessors: several of the examples used in the guide are taken from the A1 award*

- *updating assessment practice – yours or your team's – as part of continuing professional development (CPD).*

Key principles

Good practice in assessment is based on the following seven principles, which form the central themes of this guide.

1 Assessment starts with the job.

2 Assessment is holistic.

3 Assessment is judging whether evidence meets the standards.

4 Assessment means using a variety of assessment methods.

This means:

- assessing evidence resulting from the main tasks the candidate carries out in their normal workplace role.

This means:

- rather than taking an element by element approach, looking at each of the performance criteria (pc) in turn, you encourage candidates to use evidence across as many units and elements of the NVQ as possible.

This means:

- your job is to decide whether your candidates' evidence meets the standards, and nothing else.

- this is not the job of internal or external verifiers. Their job is to look at the quality of the assessment process: how you arrived at your decisions and ensuring that everyone assesses consistently.

This means:

- knowing how different assessment methods work together. Over-reliance on a particular method or using only one method can lead to unreliable decisions, based on looking at only one aspect of the candidate's competence.

5 Assessment is fair and consistent and part of the quality assurance process.

6 You use policies and procedures that minimise bureaucracy.

7 Assessment decisions are based on the evidence.

This means:

- showing the internal verifier (IV) how you've arrived at your decisions. (The internal verification process is based on trust in the assessor's decision.)

- comparing your assessment practice with that of other assessors within your centre and agreeing to change the way you do things if necessary.

This means:

- collecting and presenting evidence in a way that makes it as easy as possible for you to carry out assessment and record your decisions.

- candidates not having to store all their evidence in one place (or put together a huge portfolio full of their work where competence has to be inferred by the assessor, creating an unnecessary paper trail).

- wherever possible and practical, seeing and assessing the evidence in the place where it occurs naturally and/or is usually kept – in the workplace.

This means:

- keeping a record of all decisions in the portfolio, which should contain:

  - *the assessor's decisions,* stating who assessed what and when, what the decision was and the rationale for this, and stating where to find the evidence that underpins the decision.

  - *evidence of competence (and nothing else).* Evidence of learning or 'distance travelled' is not appropriate here.

Where this guide refers to NVQs, this includes SVQs.

Who's who in the delivery of NVQs

Qualifications and Curriculum Authority (QCA) or Scottish Qualifications Authority (SQA)

This organisation is responsible for approving and accrediting qualifications nationally.

Standards setting body (SSB) or Sector Skills Council (SSC)

These organisations develop the national occupational standards on which NVQs are based.

Awarding bodies

These are organisations approved by QCA to award NVQs. All candidates are registered with an awarding body, which awards them their certificate when they achieve their qualification.

External verifier (EV)

This is the person appointed by the awarding body to monitor the work of the approved centre. The EV acts as the link between the awarding body and the approved centre by working closely with the internal verifiers and centre manager to ensure that the quality of assessment and internal verification meets the national standard.

The approved assessment centre (managed by a centre co-ordinator or manager)

Internal verifier (IV)

This is the person appointed by the approved centre to ensure consistency and quality of the assessment process. The IV is qualified through achieving their V1 (or D34) award.

Assessor

This is you, the person responsible for working with the candidate to advise and assess them. You will have been appointed by the approved centre and be qualified through achieving or working towards your A1 (or D32/33) award.

Candidates/learners

These are individuals registered with an awarding body for NVQs, who work towards their awards through demonstrating their competence through performance in the workplace.

You will find a full explanation of the internal and external verifiers' roles in ENTO's *Excellence in assessment and verification* (Read, H., 2004).

The assessor's role

As an assessor, you need to know thoroughly both the standards for which you are assessing and the job you are assessing. This is why all assessment strategies specify the amount and type of experience expected of assessors.

Most people become assessors to use the skills they have acquired as a result of their occupational experience and expertise. If you are new to the role you also will need to develop specific skills associated with assessing, and practise them until you become confident. Similarly, if you are an experienced assessor you will find it helpful to check your performance against current best practice. Don't think that just because you're a seasoned assessor, you are necessarily performing in line with everyone else.

This section contains an overview of the assessor's job and looks at your main areas of responsibility.

What the assessor does

As the assessor, your role is to assess evidence of candidates' competence against the standards in the NVQ. In addition, you are responsible for:

- inducting the candidate into the NVQ and explaining what they need to do and identifying any additional support they may need

- planning assessments with the candidate and agreeing on the assessment methods you use with them

- carrying out assessment using a variety of methods

- providing constructive feedback to the candidate concerning his or her progress and advising on how to become competent

- recording your assessment decisions and explaining how you arrived at them

- reviewing progress with candidates and any others involved

- collecting a variety of high-quality evidence so that internal verification can be carried out effectively

- maintaining your own technical and vocational competencies in the areas you assess

- contributing to the quality assurance procedures within your centre.

Reaching an assessment decision

When you assess, your job is to decide whether or not the evidence meets the standards in question. To help you reach an assessment decision, ask yourself the following questions:

Is the evidence...

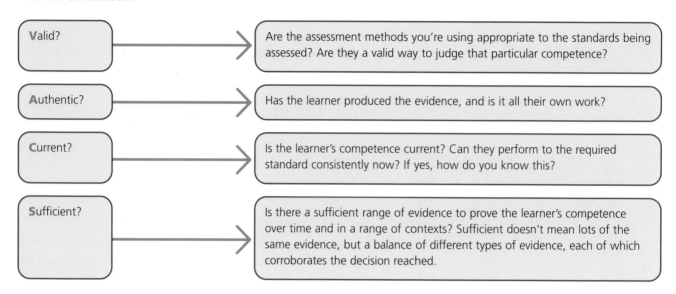

Valid? — Are the assessment methods you're using appropriate to the standards being assessed? Are they a valid way to judge that particular competence?

Authentic? — Has the learner produced the evidence, and is it all their own work?

Current? — Is the learner's competence current? Can they perform to the required standard consistently now? If yes, how do you know this?

Sufficient? — Is there a sufficient range of evidence to prove the learner's competence over time and in a range of contexts? Sufficient doesn't mean lots of the same evidence, but a balance of different types of evidence, each of which corroborates the decision reached.

When you've arrived at a decision, you also need to ask two further questions to check your own assessment practice.

Is the evidence also:

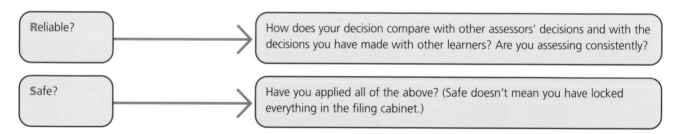

Reliable? — How does your decision compare with other assessors' decisions and with the decisions you have made with other learners? Are you assessing consistently?

Safe? — Have you applied all of the above? (Safe doesn't mean you have locked everything in the filing cabinet.)

For the learner to meet the standards in question, you must answer 'yes' confidently in each case. This is important, as you should be able to justify your decision as part of the quality assurance (verification) process. In addition, should the candidate disagree with your decision and appeal against it, you need to be able to explain how and why you reached it.

If you answer 'no' to one or more of the first four questions, this tells you that the learner is not yet competent or that you have insufficient evidence to be able to make a safe decision.

If you answer 'no' or 'I don't know' to the last two, you need to talk to your internal verifier about your centre's quality assurance procedures and how you can participate in them.

The main assessment methods

The following table shows the main methods of assessment you will use as an NVQ assessor, along with a brief explanation of each one and when to use it.

Assessment method	What this means	When to use it
Observation	Watching candidates perform in the workplace	Most SSBs specify observation as a primary or mandatory method within their assessment schemes.
Professional discussion	A conversation in which candidates describe and reflect on their performance and knowledge in relation to the requirements of the standards	One of the best ways to test the validity and reliability of a candidate's evidence. Can often be used to cover a range of work activities and units. It is an effective way to test 'deep' rather than 'superficial' learning.
Evidence from others (witness testimony)	Another person's account of what a candidate has done in the workplace and/or to confirm existing knowledge	A useful way to support observation. Can be used to confirm consistent performance over time. May be used in conjunction with APL /APE /APA (see below) to verify a candidate's claim to existing knowledge and skills.
Questioning	Using a range of questioning techniques, either spoken or written	One of the main methods used to find out whether a candidate has the necessary underpinning knowledge.
Examination of products	The outcomes or products of a candidate's work activity	Must be the result of real work. May be used in conjunction with observation, questioning or professional discussion.
Accreditation of prior learning, experience and achievement (APL/APE/APA)	Assessment of a candidate's existing level of knowledge and skill in relation to the standards	Without detailed assessment, it can be difficult to judge whether prior claims constitute valid, authentic and current evidence.
Simulation	Using a replica of the work environment to assess competence	When it is impossible for the candidate to perform in a real-life work environment.
Setting projects and assignments	Assessing the outcomes of projects and assignments that a candidate has undertaken as part of real work	May be used in conjunction with questioning or professional discussion. (Remember, though, that projects and assignments set as part of the learning process provide no evidence of competence.)
Setting tests	Formal testing of skills and/ or knowledge	Testing sometimes forms part of the requirements for independent assessment and external quality control in NVQs where there is a considerable body of underpinning knowledge of a technical nature, or safety-related knowledge and skill requirements. Testing is not widely used within NVQ assessment.

Self-check: how well do you know the assessment methods?

To help you get the most from the guide, answer the following questions honestly in relation to each of the main assessment methods.

Questions	Yes	No	Not sure	Turn to the following section
Observation				Observation, page 15
▪ Do you know what observation involves?	☐	☐	☐	
▪ Are you 100 per cent confident about using it?	☐	☐	☐	
▪ Can you record the results effectively?	☐	☐	☐	
Professional discussion				Professional discussion, page 23
▪ Have you been trained in how to use professional discussion with candidates?	☐	☐	☐	
▪ Have your candidates been trained in their role in professional discussion?	☐	☐	☐	
▪ Do you and your candidates know what to do before, during and after a professional discussion?	☐	☐	☐	
Witness testimony				Witness testimony, page 33
Do you know...				
▪ when to use contributions from other people?	☐	☐	☐	
▪ how to identify suitable witnesses?	☐	☐	☐	
▪ how to brief your witness?	☐	☐	☐	
▪ the best way to collect a witness testimony?	☐	☐	☐	
▪ what a good written contribution from another person looks like (or sounds like if it's recorded)?	☐	☐	☐	
Questioning				Questioning, page 41
Do you know...				
▪ about the different types of questions you can use?	☐	☐	☐	
▪ when to use questioning?	☐	☐	☐	
▪ what questions to ask?	☐	☐	☐	
▪ how questioning supports the other methods, and contributes to sufficiency?	☐	☐	☐	
Examination of products				Examination of products, page 47
▪ Are you confident about using evidence the candidate has produced as a result of their work?	☐	☐	☐	

Questions	Yes	No	Not sure	Turn to the following section
Other methods				
Are you confident about using the following, where appropriate:				
▪ Simulation?	☐	☐	☐	Other methods, page 57
▪ Accreditation of prior learning, experience and/or achievement?	☐	☐	☐	Other methods, page 57
▪ Tests?	☐	☐	☐	Other methods, page 57
▪ Projects and assignments?	☐	☐	☐	Other methods, page 57

If you have answered no or not sure to any of the questions, turn to the relevant section(s) in the guide first.

Making links

When carrying out assessment for NVQs, you'll need to refer to several published documents. These are the national occupational standards (NOS), assessment strategies, evidence requirements and the NVQ Code of Practice.

1. National occupational standards, assessment strategies and evidence requirements

National occupational standards (NOS)

These are written by the Sector Skills Council (SSC) or standards setting body (SSB) responsible for a particular profession or occupational area. Organisations using NOS as a way of recognising staff competence develop a strategy to ensure that assessment of the standards is uniformly managed and carried out.

Assessment strategies

NVQs are the competence-based qualifications developed from NOS. All NVQs are supported by assessment strategies written by the SSC, which dictate how the particular NVQ must be assessed, by whom and what qualifications, skills and experience the assessors and verifiers of the NVQ must have.

The main difference between NOS and NVQs is that the SSC sets the assessment strategy for an NVQ, while the assessment strategy for NOS is developed internally by the organisation.

Evidence requirements

Candidates need evidence to demonstrate their competence. Awarding bodies stipulate the evidence required for NVQs. The evidence needed for NOS is determined internally by the organisation and is not externally imposed. Whether you are working on NVQs or NOS, you need to know what evidence candidates require in order to demonstrate competence.

Although you need to know the standards and refer to them when you're planning and assessing, your starting point is the candidate's job and the tasks they do regularly:

'When I started this job, I went through all the units and elements and related them to the main activities we carry out within the store. This meant we didn't waste assessors' time.'

'At Level 3, the candidate has to make changes within customer service. You need to plan over time so that they can research needs, suggest changes, try them out and evaluate the results. You relate this to something the candidate already does within their work.'

'I look at the optional units in the NVQ. This can often be the candidate's whole job or specialism. Now that I'm more experienced, I realise that the optional units actually determine the way in which my candidate approaches the whole NVQ – the way they demonstrate the mandatory units is influenced by the optionals, so now we begin by choosing the optionals and the mandatory units follow on naturally out of these.'

2. The NVQ Code of Practice (QCA, 2002)

You also need to be aware of what constitutes good practice for NVQ assessment centres. The NVQ Code of Practice contains criteria that all centres offering NVQs must meet, including sanctions if your centre fails to meet them. (SVQs have separate guidance.)

Following a review carried out by QCA and ACCAC in 2003/4, the NVQ Code of Practice will be updated during 2006.

1 Observation

A major part of your job is to observe candidates in their work setting. Observation is the main assessment method to use in work-based learning, and most NVQ assessment strategies tell you to use it as a primary method. Because NVQs are about competence under real-life working conditions, the best way to assess candidates is by seeing them in action in the workplace. Observation is the most valid and reliable method of assessment because you can be sure that the evidence you see is both authentic and current.

This section explains when to use observation, how to plan and carry out observation sessions, and how to record your observation decisions.

When to use observation

'I assess hairdressers. I want to see how they cut hair and how they treat their clients.'

Generally, you're aiming to observe the candidate carrying out the main tasks they do as part of their job. Your starting point is the assessment strategy and evidence requirements for the NVQ: these specify what must be observed and state how many times this must be seen.

To use observation successfully, however, you need to know how to make the most of it. On its own, observation doesn't tell you enough about how the candidate performs over time and across a range of conditions, and you're unlikely to cover all the knowledge and understanding even if you use clever questioning. This means that you have to use observation in combination with other assessment methods. For example, other people's accounts can tell you about the candidate's performance over time, and product evidence could also support what you have seen.

'I assess trainers, and I use training course evaluations of the sessions I've observed, the lesson plan and any needs analysis the candidate has used in planning the session.'

'You plan what methods to use with your candidate. You have to fit round them and their jobs.'

Planning and carrying out observation

'In the past, assessors have been taught that they must stick to their plans. The trouble with this is you miss assessment opportunities that aren't part of the plan!'

1 Planning

The key to observation is to plan with your candidate in outline what you want to observe, along with the date and time, but to be flexible on the day depending on what the candidate faces at work. You also need to plan around the whole activity and include evidence that will become available after the observation so that the candidate can arrange for you to have access to this.

'If one of our tutor constables is watching a probationer, they aren't going to know what kind of call's coming in. They have to go with it.'

'I assess trainers, and you want to see more than just the presentation. You want to stick around for the whole day – see how they set the room up, how well prepared they are, and what the participants think. If the session's been put on for your benefit that doesn't tell you anything about how good they really are.'

2 During the observation

Before you start, try to put the candidate at ease. Explain to them what you'll be doing:

'I tell them, "If you see me writing or not writing, don't read anything into it about your performance".'

'I remind them about what we've planned – or they go over it with me – then I tell them to carry on as normal.'

'Make a note of anything you want to follow up. For example: "Why did you carry the task out in that order?"'

Choose a suitable point at which to question the candidate, having discussed this with them at the planning stage. If they're moving around or tackling a variety of tasks, it may make sense to question them as you go along, otherwise they could forget what they were doing and why.

3 After the observation

- Ask any supplementary questions you have at this stage, but remember that these may not provide you with the full picture: the candidate may have to provide more evidence, and you may need to go and see it if it's available.
- Give the candidate feedback on how well they've done:
- tell them which of the standards they have met
- explain which of the standards they haven't met, and why
- be specific about what happens next. You may need to go back to your original assessment plan, for example: 'I've seen you give a presentation to a group of eight, and now we have to verify your performance with other groups. For this we need a witness statement from your training manager.' (This should already be part of the overall assessment plan, but you may need to contact the candidate's manager at this point.)

Making the most of observation

'We're in an old Victorian signal box at 8:30am and I'm meant to be observing my candidate, a signalman. He arrives late, so we've got 45 minutes to wait before I can observe him deal with the next train. You think: what can I do? You start a conversation and ask him about his job. You're thinking: "Knowledge and understanding: let's see his paperwork, then ask him some questions about procedures." Now he's digging out his health and safety policies and I'm asking him questions about how they apply.'

When enough is enough

Knowing when you've seen enough can sometimes be difficult. If you've agreed a half-day session, you may feel obliged to stay until the end, but the standards should be your main guide.

Self-check: gathering enough evidence

This checklist will help you decide when you've gained enough evidence.

Have I seen evidence that...	Yes	No
all the relevant pcs have been covered?	☐	☐
the range/scope of performance conditions has been covered?	☐	☐
the underpinning knowledge and understanding have been covered (by questioning or other methods)?	☐	☐
that this person performs consistently to the standards?	☐	☐

You are aiming for yes in each case.

Recording and providing an audit trail

'I came across an example of assessment by observation where the assessor simply stated that he "observed the candidate take on duties" with no further detail or evidence. He then made the decision that the candidate was competent. As his internal verifier, I couldn't agree with his decision.'

It's not enough to make a decision as the result of observation. You have to be able to explain how and why you arrived at it so that you can give feedback to the candidate on their performance, and for quality purposes. This is why the internal verifier quoted above took issue with the assessor: it isn't that the assessor didn't know what he was observing, it's that he didn't explain how he arrived at his decision or the evidence he saw to back it up.

Recording assessment decisions

You need to keep formal records of all your assessment decisions. A record of assessment is a formal document that describes:

- how the evidence has met the standards (you need to refer to the elements, pcs and knowledge)
- where you saw the evidence if it was in the workplace
- the assessment methods you used
- the date and time of your assessment.

The record can take the form of a witness testimony, professional discussion, observation or all three: it depends on the evidence requirements of the NVQ you are assessing. The main thing is to record your assessment decision – whether or not the standards were met – on each one.

The example overleaf shows how one assessor recorded his observation of an A1 candidate assessor giving feedback to a call centre candidate. The report includes his assessment decision.

ASSESSMENT REPORT

Candidate name: Ceris Jones

Date of assessment: 12 March 2006

Location of assessment: CELTAX

Assessor: Tim Dyson

NVQ: L&D Level 3

Relevant assessment plan(s): 1,2,3

Time: 11.30am

Units/elements assessed: A1.3

The standard being observed is A1.3: Give feedback to candidates on their performance

Observation of performance

During this assessment, I observed you undertaking the following work activities and made the following judgements regarding your performance, matched to the relevant standards.

	Unit	Element/ Range Knowledge
Ceris found a quiet workstation to provide her candidate with feedback from her observation. She sat next to her and explained what she had observed. She told her that she had demonstrated effective call handling skills using the required methods to initiate a call.	A1	A1.3 A 3/6/18 B
She was positive with her candidate when discussing her call handling technique, describing which areas she had achieved against the standards.		11/12/13/24 25
Ceris primarily discussed what criteria had been met, then explained which parts of the unit had not been covered. She asked questions on areas she needed to clarify and recorded the outcomes on a separate sheet.		C D
Ceris told her candidate how much more confident she sounded when making a call than on her previous observation. Ceris asked the candidate if she agreed with the feedback on her observation and if she had any questions. She answered the candidate's question on what still needed to be covered. Ceris explained that by asking her candidate some questions on what the she had done, some more outcomes had been covered. She explained that her witness testimony from her supervisor covered another of the outcomes that had not been achieved by the observation.		E F
Ceris told her candidate she would carry out another observation to cover the complaint-handling section of the qualification.		
Her candidate fully agreed with her observation record and the follow-up actions. She signed and dated the form and wrote her own feedback, which was positive, and clarified her understanding of what still needed to be covered.		

Were all performance criteria met during the observation?

Yes

The assessor describes what he sees and relates this to A1.3. In this way, all assessment decisions can be traced back to the evidence provided by the candidate (in this case, directly observed performance evidence).

The assessor makes the decision to award the candidate assessor with the standards in question on the basis of his observation.

Assessor Signature

Tim Dyson

Date 12 March 2006

Candidate Signature

Ceris Jones

Date 12 March 2006

The example shows you one way of recording observations and is for illustrative purposes only. If you are observing over a period of time, your reports will be longer and cover more of the standards. The skill of observing is to report what you see: since candidates won't perform tasks in the same order as the standard, you must relate their performance to the standards as they go along.

Myths about observation

Here are some myths that have grown up around observation and what assessors say about them:

Myth 1: Be unobtrusive

'I went into a travel agent's and the assessor was sitting on a sofa just inside the door. I had to ask her if she could see anything at all when the action was behind the counter.'

'Sometimes you need to follow the candidate around from place to place all day. You have to gauge it as you go along.'

'You don't need an inflatable Swiss cheese plant to hide behind!'

'I check with the candidate or their colleagues that where I'm sitting's OK. One time I sat down, started making notes and found I was in the boss's chair!'

'Blend in. Be a participant if you're observing a trainer, or sit with the others around the table if you're in a meeting.'

Myth 2: Be a fly on the wall

'I'm of the view that the assessment method needs to work for the candidate. If they're comfortable giving a rationale for why they're doing the task or a running commentary, that provides high-quality evidence and avoids the need for questioning later on. Plan it with them and include it in your observation.'

'You can interrupt! Otherwise the moment will pass and you'll miss the assessment opportunity. The skill is to pick your moment.'

Myth 3: Keep a written record against the pcs

'As an IV, I get sick of reading through pages and pages of observations. What I want is a whole picture with examples of what the candidate has done.'

Myth 4: Stick to the assessment plan

'I'm not saying you shouldn't plan what you're going to assess, but you need to be flexible, depending on what you see going on in front of you.'

'I was observing the candidate carrying out routine procedures when an emergency call came in. I found myself assessing a completely different unit of the NVQ.'

2 Professional discussion

Professional discussion is an in-depth, two-way conversation between the assessor and the candidate. It's the main method to use when you're assessing complex tasks and the candidate's ability to show and apply knowledge.

There are no hard and fast rules for conducting a professional discussion: much depends on how you respond to what your candidate says and your skill in moving the discussion forward if necessary. However, such discussions work best when you both know what you will be discussing, and when the candidate has had enough time to prepare and so feels relaxed about talking to you.

This section will help you plan, conduct and capture the results of professional discussions with your candidates.

'I'm not a doctor or a solicitor – how can I take part in a professional discussion?'

'Will I get any letters after my name if I'm observed doing a professional discussion?'

'Professional discussion – it's about the candidate showing off what they can do, isn't it?'

Planning the discussion

'90 per cent of a successful professional discussion is down to preparing and training the candidate and the assessor.'

Before carrying out a professional discussion you will need to plan it so that the candidate agrees with the timing of it and what they want to achieve. This planning stage is crucial and requires time and effort from both you and your candidate. You need to plan with the candidate what they will be talking about and identify anything they need to bring with them to support their claim to competence.

Self-check: preparing for professional discussion

Here are some of the things you need to do to prepare. Use the checklist to help you identify what needs to be done with your candidate at the planning stage. You are both aiming for a row of ticks.

Assessor	✓	Candidate	✓
Have I checked the evidence requirements and assessment strategy to ensure that:		Do I know the topics I will be expected to discuss and how these relate to the standards?	☐
▪ everything is covered?	☐		
▪ professional discussion is the appropriate method to use?	☐		
Am I sure this candidate is ready to be assessed?	☐	Do I know what products or examples of my work I need to bring with me to the discussion?	☐
Have I decided how this professional discussion will be used in combination with other methods (like observation and examining product evidence?)	☐	Do I have I enough time to prepare?	☐
Have I explained to the candidate that I'll be listening for their real experience in the workplace?	☐	Am I confident about taking part in a professional discussion?	☐
Have we agreed a time and place to meet?	☐	Have we agreed a time and place to meet?	☐

During the discussion

1 Put your candidate at ease

It's easy to forget that, for most candidates, professional discussion is something of an ordeal. They may be very good at their jobs but not confident about talking to an assessor. When you begin, it's important for your candidate to feel relaxed, so build this in to your practice. One way of doing this is to talk to your candidate beforehand about what to expect (see note 2 below).

2 Lay ground rules and explain them before you start

'I say: "It's OK to ask me questions if you lose your thread."'

'I explain that I may make notes, but that this isn't a reflection on them – it's my aide-memoire!'

'I tell them about the recording equipment.'

'I remind them about sticking to their real experiences and not "talking theory".'

'I tell them I'm going to stop them when we've covered the topic in enough depth.'

3 Encourage, focus and move on

Your job is to keep up the pace of the discussion and to steer it where necessary. This means encouraging your candidate to keep talking when they're on the right track; keeping them focused on the standards and moving them on when they've covered the topic in enough depth.

To encourage them, use active listening skills such as nodding or saying, 'Tell me more...'

To move them on, use specific questions such as, 'I'd like you to talk about the main methods of assessment you used. Why did you choose them?' Don't be afraid to interrupt if they wander off the point. Say something like, 'Can I interrupt you?' and follow it with a specific prompt question. (See Questioning on page 41 for more on this.)

4 Identify further opportunities

Listen for anything your candidate says that may provide further evidence of their performance, and ask to see it (or talk to those involved).

5 Bring it to a close

Give a clear signal: say something like, 'That's great. I think we can end it there.'

After the discussion

When you've finished, your candidate will want to know how well they've done, and it's your job to tell them. When you do this, follow the general principles for giving feedback.[1] After a professional discussion, you may both want to take a break, particularly if you've been involved in a long conversation. This allows you to gather your thoughts before making your final decisions and to be clear about anything that the candidate needs to do as a result. (This is definitely advisable if you're new to assessing.)

Next steps

Agree on what the candidate needs to do next, such as:

- providing further evidence, particularly if you've identified any new sources or they haven't met all the standards in question. Be specific about what they need to bring or do in relation to the standards.

- identifying and arranging to speak to potential witnesses if you think their evidence needs further corroboration.

- arranging to observe the candidate where necessary.

Record these as action points and agree them with the candidate, along with timescales.

[1] Refer to *Excellence in assessment and verification* for more on giving feedback (Read, H., 2004. Distributed by ENTO).

Recording and providing an audit trail

'I prefer to go in with a blank sheet and make notes as we go.'

There is no prescribed approach to how you structure or record the outcomes of a professional discussion. Your guiding principles are to approach it in a holistic way, with a well-prepared candidate.

The example on the next page shows one possible framework that you could adapt according to the award (or units within an award) that you're assessing. The example is based on Unit A1, where the evidence requirements prescribe professional discussion for elements A1.2, A1.3 and the knowledge requirements. In this example the assessor has structured the discussion to include A1.1, but you could extend it to cover other aspects of the evidence requirements. (You would need to carry out a similar exercise for A.1.2 and A1.3 and the associated knowledge; this is just to give you an idea.)

You can give candidates a similar framework for preparing their discussion, and an example is shown on page 29.

Assessor's framework

Tape counter	Candidates need to describe and discuss these topic areas	For assessor use	Performance criterion (pc)	Knowledge reference	Met ✓	Met by other evidence (state type & location)
	Assessment planning Describe the four assessment methods you have selected across your three plans and explain why you think these are valid, reliable and fair indicators of competence	Candidate lists the four methods they have used (one of which must be observation). Discusses the validity, reliability and fairness of the assessment methods used in relation to the type of evidence /activity being assessed, relevant aspects of the standards used and the requirements of the assessment strategy.	A1.1 c d e A.1 k	1 3 4 5 9 17 19 31 1 3 16		
	Describe how and why you have planned to involve other people in the assessment process and their precise contribution	Candidate should include the use of witnesses and possibly other people involved in the learning /assessment process, e.g. line manager, workplace supervisor, colleagues, tutor or trainer.				

Assessor comments/notes

Candidate .... Signature.. Date.............................

Assessor... Signature.. Date.............................

Candidate's framework

Tape counter	You will need to discuss these topic areas	For assessor use	Performance criterion (pc)	Knowledge reference
	Assessment planning			
	State the four assessment methods you have selected across your three plans and describe why you consider these to be valid, reliable and fair indicators of competence		A1.1 c d e	1 3 4 5 9 17 19 31
	Describe how and why you have planned to involve other people in the assessment process and their precise contribution		A.1 k	1 3 16

Notes

The blank page approach

When recording the results of professional discussion, experienced assessors often choose the 'blank page' approach. This means recording what the candidate says as they go along, rather than taking a straight-line approach through the framework. They said:

'It relies on your professionalism and judgement as the assessor.'

'It's natural and realistic.'

'You can listen to the candidate.'

'The candidate leads – and that's what you're looking for, especially at levels 3 and 4.'

However, this approach assumes an in-depth knowledge of both the standards and how they are assessed, so if you are new to this method of assessing you may want to use your framework to check that you are covering everything while the discussion unfolds, and until you are confident about using it.

Myths about professional discussion

Here are some myths that have grown up around professional discussion and what assessors say about them:

Myth 1: You have to write down what the candidate says

'Nope! You can record it. I take a digital voice recorder wherever I go. You have to refer to the answers the candidate gives that show competence, though. I make notes throughout.'

Myth 2: You can't ask a question, particularly if the candidate's in full flow

'Of course you can – particularly if you can't reach your decision without the answer.'

'If the candidate refers to a particular piece of work I might say 'show me' and we'd go and have a look at it.'

Myth 3: Professional discussion is a matter of common sense

'The question you need to ask is: are your assessors and candidates trained in how to use this method? As someone who trains assessors, in my experience the answer's usually "no".'

Myth 4: The candidate needs to look the part

'You're assessing what they know and can do – not what they look like!'

'I was so worried I bought myself a new suit.' Candidate assessor

Myth 5: You have to give feedback straight away

'It's a matter of personal preference. Fine if you know what you're going to say, but I find it useful to gather my thoughts after a two-hour discussion. I tell the candidate in outline, then give them a ring or arrange to see them a bit later.'

3 Witness testimony

Witness testimonies are other people's accounts of what your candidate can do. Since you can't be there all the time to observe candidates in action, you can make use of a good witness, who can tell you a lot about how a candidate performs over a period of time and under different conditions.

As a supplement to observation, evidence from others in the form of witness testimonies works well. You can use witness testimony to check that candidates perform to the standards consistently over time.

This section tells you when to use witness testimony, how to identify and brief potential witnesses, and the different ways of recording a witness's account so that it constitutes valid evidence of competence.

When to use witness testimony

Your own observation will yield only a snapshot of how a candidate performs on the day you visit; an appropriate witness can tell you about other occasions when the candidate has carried out the activity you've observed. Witness testimony is also useful when the outcomes of a candidate's work are brief or transitory, and it's difficult for you to be in the right place at the right time to see them perform. Reliable accounts from other people will confirm that your candidate:

- **performs consistently when carrying out important, routine procedures**
  (for example, disposing of waste correctly; making good use of resources; following health and safety procedures at all times)

- **deals with a one-off occurrence competently**
  (for example, an emergency; a customer problem; an annual stock-take)

- **performs in situations where confidentiality or sensitivity is an issue**
  (for example, giving confidential advice and guidance; bathing an elderly service user within a care home; giving someone a massage at a health spa).

Flexibility is the key: with your candidate, you'll need to identify who will make the best witness, while also keeping an open mind when you're observing or as a result of professional discussions about who else who might be suitable.

'I get permission from one of the hotel guests, then ask them how the receptionist dealt with them as part of my observation.'

'I get their office manager to observe them carrying out key admin tasks over a two-week period.'

'If they've been working with someone else, I ask if I can talk to that person.'

Identifying potential witnesses

It's best to identify people who may be able to act as witnesses during the assessment planning process. Generally, they need to be people who work with the candidate and who are in a position to observe their performance on a regular basis. They might be a colleague, a supervisor, a trainer or a manager.

Witness checklist

Ask your candidate:

	Yes	No
▪ Can the person observe you in the workplace?	☐	☐
▪ Do they work with you on a regular basis?	☐	☐
▪ Do they know the requirements of your job?	☐	☐
▪ Can they comment on whether or not you are performing well?	☐	☐
▪ Would they be willing to act as your witness?	☐	☐

You are aiming for a yes in each case.

Remember...

1 Explain to your candidate what witness testimony involves. Once they understand how another person's account may be used in their assessment, they can take advantage of any unplanned opportunities that crop up at work.

2 It's important for you to gain the potential witness's commitment, as you may be asking them to write a report or to comment in detail.

3 Don't use other NVQ candidates as witnesses: they won't possess the necessary competence.

Briefing witnesses

Once you've identified a suitable witness, you need to brief them about what's involved. If you tell the person exactly what you want them to do beforehand, you will save time and trouble, and you're more likely to get a meaningful account.

Overall, you're asking them to provide an objective account of what the candidate can do. This means:

- using their own words and the active voice ('I have seen Dawn...' rather than 'It was noted...' or similar)

- being objective: sticking to what they see the candidate do, rather than commenting on the kind of person they are and/or making value judgements; avoiding, for example 'Narinder is very good with customers and produced an excellent report.'

- describing what the candidate does: the work task(s), the context and conditions, and their timescales and/or frequency, all of which need to be based in the workplace

- referring to any records, policies and procedures and where these are located

- referring to the outcomes of the work the candidate does (a roof, a sill, a painted wall, a haircut, a report, etc.) and where these can be seen, if appropriate.

Ask them to sign and date their account and to give you their contact details so that you can follow it up if you need to.

The ad hoc witness

Ad hoc witnesses form a vital part of assessment. These are the people who are essential to a candidate's job, such as clients, hotel guests, customers and telephone callers. They can't be contacted in advance, yet if they are there on the day you assess they can corroborate what's taken place and help you reach your assessment decision. As the assessor, you need to identify appropriate opportunities within your occupational area to talk to ad hoc witnesses.

Reliability

To ensure that a witness is reliable, it makes sense to find out about their experience and competence. Some assessment strategies clearly state who can and can't act as a witness. This may mean asking the person to give details of their experience and/or qualifications.

Recording and providing an audit trail

On the opposite page is an example of a written witness testimony for a candidate assessor working towards the A1 standards.

Witness testimony

Justin Hough A1 Candidate

Following our telephone conversation about Justin's work in our centre I can confirm that he commenced work as an assessor in our centre on 1 September 2005. Since then he has participated in scheduled standardisation meetings which have included evidence from his allocated candidates. Evidence of this is maintained in our centre records and will be available to you as agreed when you visit.

I am also happy to confirm that Justin has consistently met the requirements of our internal quality assurance procedures. His assessments have been consistent with the assessment strategy for the qualification and his assessment work complies with our internal assessment and verification policies. In particular, he has used our standard documentation throughout all of his assessment work, including the use of assessment plans, assessment records, records of reviews and records of assessment decisions and feedback.

All documentation has been properly completed and appropriately filed. Sampling of his work through our internal sampling procedures has shown that in completing documentation he has created adequate audit trails that enable candidate progress and achievement to be tracked from the document-ation in candidate portfolios back to the centre records and vice versa.

Again, as mentioned above, all of this can be confirmed by examination of our centre records, which will be available to you when you visit.

Finally, I can confirm that all of our centre policies and procedures in relation to safety, health and environment have been complied with and also that centre policies relating to the handling of personal data/ confidentiality and equal opportunity have been complied with at all times.

I trust that the above is adequate for your needs, but if you require further information or clarification please do not hesitate to contact me.

Signed: G. Walker

Date: 14 March 2006

Title: Internal Verifier and Centre Co-ordinator

The statement in this paragraph helps to meet the requirements for element A1.4, but doesn't provide sufficient evidence in itself: you need to examine the evidence in the workplace. This is an opportunity to combine assessment methods. While looking at the evidence in the workplace you could have a discussion with the witness or the candidate, or both, asking appropriate questions.

Remember that when evidence is left in the workplace your assessment records must say where this is kept.

Again, remember to look at these.

Here, the witness confirms the candidate's competence over time in areas of policy and procedures.

The rest of the statement also provides evidence for element A1.4. You would need to examine these products to meet the requirements of other parts of the standard, and again these could be left in the workplace and discussed with the candidate and witness as necessary. This will also give you the opportunity to see how the documentation has met quality assurance requirements by asking the candidate to 'walk you through' the centre's systems and procedures.

Be prepared to contact the witness and question them further, even if they don't offer.

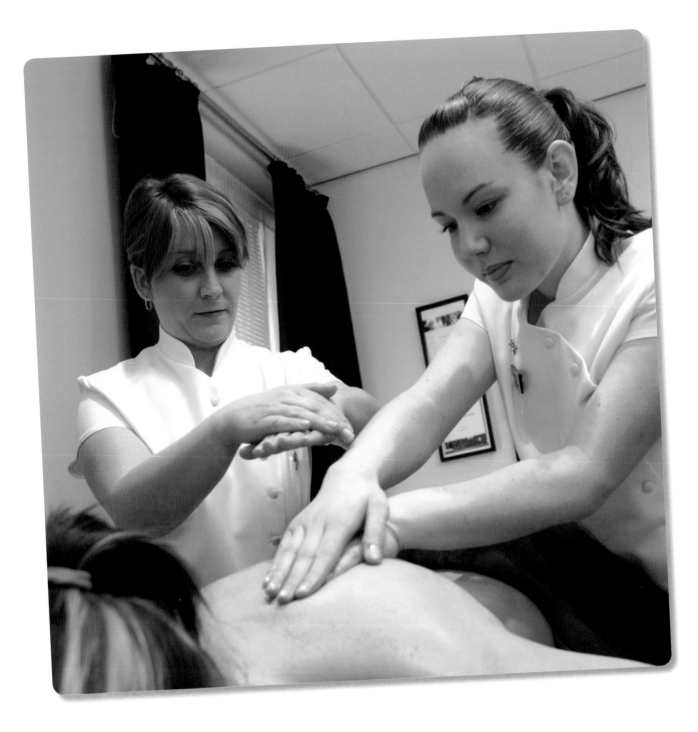

You don't always have to use a written account from the witness. Other ways of recording are:

- a taped interview of you, the assessor, questioning the witness

- a video taken by the witness with his or her spoken comments

- writing down the witness's account over the phone. If your witness isn't happy to take notes, they can always ring you during their observation and ask you to write down what they are seeing. You can then ask them to read through what you wrote and sign and date it if they feel it is an accurate account of what took place.

If you haven't talked to the witness directly, be prepared to follow up their testimony with questioning, either face-to-face or over the telephone.

Myths about witness testimony

Here are some of the myths about using witness testimony and what other assessors say:

Myth 1: Your witness needs to know what's being assessed

'In my experience the best witnesses don't always know the standards.'

Myth 2: The witness needs to be someone in authority

'Not necessarily: customers, peers or colleagues make excellent witnesses. On the other hand, fellow NVQ candidates make unreliable witnesses and definitely shouldn't be used.'

Myth 3: The witness should always be prepared in advance

'I make a point of asking a customer how they have been treated by the candidate. You can't ask them in advance – you ask them on the spot.'

Myth 4: You should transcribe any recorded testimony

'Recording is fine, provided you refer to the appropriate part of the tape/CD/disc, etc. in relation to the standards achieved.'

Myth 5: The candidate can write the witness testimony and get the person to sign it

'Definitely not: that's not valid. But you can get the candidate to write a report and ask the witness to comment on it and countersign it. That way you can check that the witness has read through it in detail.'

Myth 6: The witness's say-so and signature are proof that the candidate is competent

'Only the assessor can judge whether or not the candidate has met the standards – otherwise you wouldn't need the assessor.'

4 Questioning

Assessors use questioning to explore candidates' implied performance. You may not observe them performing under all the conditions laid down in the standards, but with careful questioning you can find out what they do under those conditions. Even if you haven't seen them do an activity, you can still find out whether they know enough about how to carry it out.

This section explains when to use questioning and describes a variety of different questioning techniques. It also tells you how to capture your candidate's answers so that they form meaningful evidence of performance or underpinning knowledge.

'Asking the right questions comes when you know the job and the standards. It becomes second nature because if you don't see something, you automatically know you have to follow it up with questioning.'

'You won't be there to see your candidate disposing of the toner cartridge correctly. You have to ask them what they would do, or ask someone else who sees them do it.'

When to use questioning

Questioning goes hand in hand with observation, and is an integral part of professional discussion and witness testimony. You also use questioning to establish a candidate's knowledge and understanding, and to plug gaps in your knowledge of their competence, when you have already used one of the main assessment methods.

Following an observation of performance, you can use questions in a number of ways:

- **to clarify your candidate's response to things that happened during the observation**

  'I couldn't hear everything when you answered the telephone. Could you tell me what the other person said to you?'

- **to establish why they did (or didn't) do something in a particular way**

  'Why did you increase the heat?'

- **to find out how they would have dealt with unforeseen events had they occurred**

  'What would you have done if the customer had said no?'

- **to find out how they would modify their approach to a task when working in a different context**

  'What would you have done if you'd been working with oak?'

Questioning techniques

Assessors can use various types of question in different ways, depending on the sort of information you need from your candidate. You can use:

- open questions

- closed questions

- probing questions

- hypothetical (what if?) questions.

'If I come in on the middle of a job, I know I've got to ask questions about what went before – things like their choice of materials, how they ordered them, and how they planned and costed the job. This is all part of the underpinning knowledge, but it comes naturally when you talk about the task.'

Open questions

Open questions usually include the words:

why   *what*   *where*   *how*   *who*   *when*

You can use open questions to encourage candidates to give a detailed explanation or when you want more than a one-word answer. For example:

'Tell me why it is important to carry out this task in the correct sequence.'

'Explain to me how you…'

Closed questions

Closed questions require a short or one-word answer such as 'Yes', 'No' or 'the red one'. Using closed questions can help you:

▪ check facts – for example, 'Do you normally start work at this time?'

▪ ensure that you have understood correctly – for example, 'Have you been carrying out this task for three months?'

▪ take control of the conversation. For example, when closing down an over-talkative candidate you might say, 'OK, let's stop there, shall we?

Probing questions

Probing questions are follow-up questions, to ask when you want to find out more. You can use them to:

▪ extract more detailed information about the candidate's knowledge and experience

▪ probe broad statements a candidate may have made in the course of a previous answer

▪ get beyond any superficial or rehearsed answers to questions.

Probing questions use the answer you receive from one question as the basis for taking the discussion further with your next question. For example:

'You said that you carried out the usual health and safety checks. What did that involve?'

'Can you give me an example?'

'You briefly described… Can you tell me more about that?'

'Could you say a little more about…?'

Reflecting back the candidate's exact words is a useful way of framing a probing question. For example, 'You say you had difficulty in that situation… ?'

Probing is more than a request for further information. To probe effectively, you need to:

▪ compare what the candidate says with the way they say it. If there are inconsistencies, follow up with further questioning

▪ keep asking supplementary questions, focusing on the points the candidate raises, until you get to the detail you require.

Hypothetical questions

Hypothetical questions are those that use or imply the words 'What if..?'. You can use them to establish your candidate's ability to cope with contingencies, rare and unusual occurrences, or emergency situations. It is sometimes a mandatory form of questioning in some assessment strategies when performance evidence is unlikely to be available.

Be careful when using hypothetical questions. They ask candidates to imagine how they might behave in a particular scenario or situation, whereas you are looking for what they would actually do. This applies particularly to complex scenarios or situations. When using hypothetical questions in complex situations it's best to take the candidate through the scenario incrementally and ask questions about one stage at a time.

Examples

Here are some examples of hypothetical questions.

Health and safety

What action would you take if you found yourself in a situation where the operator was not following correct health and safety procedures?

How would you check that he or she had been given up to-date information about the hazards and risks involved in the job?

How would you confirm that he or she had been given relevant training?

Having established the facts, what recommendation could you make to the manager?

Travel

What must you consider when booking a hotel room for a customer who uses a wheelchair?

What should you organise for your customer if they make a late holiday booking and there is not sufficient time for the tickets to be sent to their home in time for their flight?

What should you do if a customer returns from their holiday and tells you that their holiday was completely spoilt because it rained all the time, and now they want a refund?

A word of warning...

As an assessor, you should avoid leading questions because they reveal nothing about the candidate and can give you a false impression of their abilities. It's easy to fall into the trap of using leading questions without meaning to. Leading questions are phrased in such a way that the answer is obvious:

'You wouldn't do it that way, would you?'

'So, you find that aspect of the job relatively straightforward?'

This can sometimes happen if you've arrived at a premature decision about the candidate's competence and you ask the kind of question that can only confirm your decision.

Written questions

Some assessment strategies allow you to use written questions, and these can be useful if time is of the essence and/or you have candidates spread over a wide geographical area. However, giving a written set of questions to all candidates as a matter of course is poor practice. Written questions should be as individual as the candidate and their circumstances. As an assessment method, you should use it to capture knowledge that has not been demonstrated or proved in other ways.

'I had a list of "What would you do if...?" written questions to fill in. Writing's not my strong point and it took me ages.'

'My assessor left me two sheets of questions with boxes down the side. I had to tick if I was doing it or not. Of course, I said I was!'

'We sat down as a group and filled in the questions together.'

'I told my manager it was OK to help with my work, so I asked her the questions and wrote down her answers.'

Recording and providing an audit trail

Candidates will refer to all kinds of potential evidence during the course of questioning. Your job is to show how their answers form meaningful evidence of performance or underpinning knowledge, and to capture this when you're reaching and recording your assessment decisions.

For example, if the candidate refers to relevant company procedures during questioning, ask questions about how they are used, then ask to see the procedures. Record the fact that you have seen them and where they are kept as part of your assessment decision against the relevant standards.

'I make notes during questioning. I tell the candidate I'm going to do it beforehand and I try and do it when there's a natural break in the conversation, but if the candidate says something important, I may stop them and write down their answer. I use it as part of the explanation of my assessment decision.'

Myths about questioning

Here are some myths that have grown up around questioning and what assessors say about them:

Myth 1: Candidates have to get the answers right

'Right and wrong doesn't come into it. You're looking for evidence against the standards in the context of the candidate's work.'

'The worst example I've come across is the assessor who used a list of pre-prepared questions and answers. If the candidate's answer didn't compare favourably, he or she was marked as incorrect and not awarded the standards. This approach takes no account of the candidate's individual circumstances and knowledge.'

Myth 2: Candidates have to get the answers *and* their spelling right

'I've seen assessors who red-pen candidates' written answers.'

'You're not assessing their literacy.'

5 Examination of products

Product evidence is anything the candidate produces as a result of their work. Examining products isn't strictly an assessment method, because you're looking at the outcomes or end product of candidates' performance (as opposed to watching them actually do something). However, this forms an important part of the assessor's job because you can't always be there to observe a candidate in action, so examining product evidence can help you build up a picture of the candidate's overall competence.

This section tells you about the different types of product that may be used as evidence, and how to make the most of this type of evidence when you are examining it to help you assess competence.

What is product evidence?

Examples of product evidence can be things like:

- invoices

- plans

- reports

- budgets

- items that the candidate has made (photographed or videoed if the item is big).

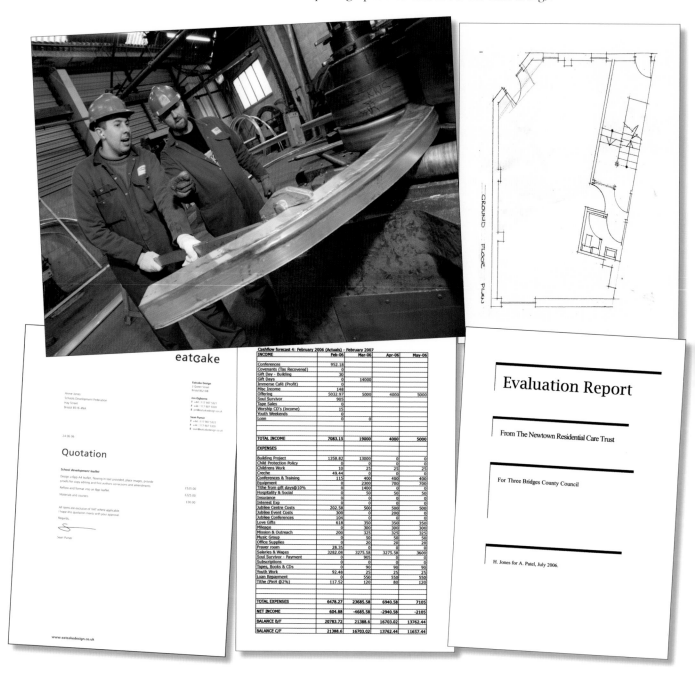

In some cases the outcomes of candidates' work are concrete (a report, a decorated room, a tiled roof, a door that's been hung or a plumbed-in central heating system). In other cases the outcomes aren't as obvious (a satisfied customer, a nutritious meal), or may only happen occasionally (a stock take, or changing suppliers).

Recording and providing an audit trail

When assessing and recording product evidence, you must bear in mind two things:

- On their own, products aren't evidence of competence. You need to assess them using the main assessment methods, for example:
  - observing the candidate producing them
  - using another's account of how they were produced or how they meet the standards
  - asking how and why they were produced as part of a professional discussion
  - using questioning to establish the candidate's underpinning knowledge of how and why the products were produced.
- All the products that the candidate shows you must be the result of the work they carry out. You can't set them a special task to cover certain standards, for example, and shouldn't set a task covered by their normal work.

'Product evidence is another way the candidate can show me their competence. I combine this with, say, the observation I have done, to corroborate competence and fill in gaps. This is triangulation of evidence, and assessors in our centre always use at least one other assessment method with product evidence for reliability.'

Making the most of product evidence

On the next few pages are three examples of product evidence, each one accompanied by a table showing how the evidence relates to the Learning and Development (L&D) standards. These weren't the only evidence of the candidate's performance, but give an idea of how product evidence helps to build up a picture of a candidate's competence.

The three types of product evidence were submitted by a candidate working towards the Level 4 L&D standards. She concentrated on tasks that were directly relevant to her role as a staff development manager. The tasks were:

- identifying staff development needs in relation to the organisation's aims and contractual obligations
- setting up a programme of staff development to enable staff to gain their Level 3 Direct Trainers Award, key skills and to assess using APL and APE.

Product one is part of her action plan for staff development and for her Level 4 qualification (the complete plan covers an 18-month period). Product two is part of a series of PowerPoint slides introducing the staff development programme. Product three is an extract from the company's guide to APL/APE/APA for assessors.

Product one: level 4 action plan

L&D LEVEL 4

Key action points	By whom	Timescale	Further action	Done
Collate details of training needs analysis and ensure that staff are entered at the correct level for the L&D qualification	The candidate	April	Ensure that all reports are returned by managers to be collated for development	☐
Register candidates for levels 3 and 4	The candidate	April	Provide administration department with candidates' details	☐
Plan training content with other trainers	The candidate and trainers	May	Check trainers' capability and confidence to provide relevant training	☐
Agree individual learning/training plans with staff	The candidate and staff	May	Provide training schedules for staff	☐
Book accommodation and facilities for training	The candidate	May	Work out numbers, meal arrangements and costs	☐
Draw up assessment plans and schedules with assessors and internal verifiers	The candidate, the assessors and IVs	May	Work out assessment schedules	☐
Check training material with trainers against the standards (including pcs & range) for initial staff training	The candidate	End June	Map training content to relevant L&D unit	☐
Draw up internal verification plan	The candidate	End June	Work out internal verification schedule and sampling strategy	☐
Provide additional assistance for the assessment team	The candidate	Mid June	Provide staff with help gathering relevant evidence	☐
Completion of initial units by staff	The candidate and staff	July	Ensure that portfolios are assessed for completion of unit, then iv'd	☐
Develop and complete training	The candidate	July	Complete training packs	☐
Check training material with trainers against the standards (including pcs & range) for Session 2 training	The candidate and trainers	August	Map training content to relevant L&D units	☐
Session 2 training	The candidate	September	Provide staff with training packs	☐
Review progression of training material for Session 3 training	The candidate	September	Map training content to relevant L&D units	☐
Session 3 training	The candidate	November	Provide staff with training packs; review progress	☐

This product evidence was used for these units:	The assessor also used these assessment methods:
L4 Design learning programmes L5 Agree learning programmes with learners L8 Manage the contribution of other people to the learning process	▪ Professional discussion ▪ Observation of the staff development manager agreeing a learning programme with a member of staff, followed by questioning of the candidate's underpinning knowledge ▪ Witness testimony from other trainers describing their contribution

Product two: presentation slides

AIMS TRAINING

LEVEL 3
DIRECT TRAINING
AND SUPPORT

DEVELOPMENT PROGRAMME

Introduction

- Why has AIMS introduced a staff development programme?

- To introduce minimum standards in professional qualifications, so that our clients benefit from working with a well- trained partner providing a quality service

Key development areas

- Training design and delivery
- APL
- Key skills

Benefits

- Consistency in the quality of training delivery
- Improved assessing and coaching skills
- Structured lesson plans identifying and meeting learning outcomes
- Competence in recognising and maximising APL/APE/APA credits
- Staff motivation and satisfaction

Staff development

Two routes:

- Academic route: teaching hours and essays
- NVQ work-based route: on the job, planning and delivery, observations, meetings

Staff development

What level ?

- Level 3 will be compulsory for assessors/trainers and the resource development team.
- Level 4 will be compulsory for the management team.

This product evidence was used for these units:	The assessor also used these assessment methods:
L2 Identify the learning and development needs of the organisation	▪ Professional discussion, to establish how needs were identified
G2 Contributing to learning within the organisation	▪ Observation of training delivery and questioning on how the training would be covered
L13 Enabling group learning	▪ Observation of the staff development manager giving the presentation to staff, followed by questioning of the candidate's underpinning knowledge of training and learning

The Recycle Training Company

The APA/APE/APL Guide to the Administration Framework

Introduction

At Recycle Training, learners may join their training programme having already spent time working in the retail industry. They may have also previously achieved industry qualifications that can be used to accredit them with APA/APE/APL against relevant parts of their current training programme.

This information needs to be covered with learners at induction before they start their training programmes. At the initial visit, the assessor needs to identify with the learner their previous experience and qualifications.

The quality assurance administration team is responsible for tracking and checking any achievements from information received from learners. It is not their role to agree or make recommendations for learning plans or to accredit this information towards the learners' training programmes.

This guide will raise your awareness of:

- what APA/APE/APL is

- your role

- the procedure for recording this information at Recycle Training.

What is APA?

Accreditation of prior achievement (APA) is the term used when candidates use evidence from previous achievements as credits for their competence.

Assessors sometimes lack expertise in this area of assessment. As an A1 assessor you are required to have the skills to be able to accredit prior achievements against the NVQ framework and also to be able to identify and recognise credits for proxy qualifications.

You also need to consider any credits that can be used against the Advanced Apprenticeship (AA) framework. The framework is detailed in section 4. Learners may not be aware or understand that their prior achievements may be used as a credit towards their training programme.

Once we have established that a learner has achieved an industry qualification, such as an advanced GNVQ in Customer Service, careful consideration is given to the level at which the learner will enter the programme. For this, we need to establish how the qualification they hold is accredited against their NVQ framework.

Recycle Training works closely with the learner's employer to ensure that they understand the requirements of the framework and provide them with information so that they recruit learners who will be able to progress and achieve an AA.

The IV in conjunction with the employer will take into consideration the learner's industry qualifications, GCSE grades, NVQ qualifications, key skills and performance at the selection and recruitment process.

Achievements have to be verified in the form of authenticated evidence. We would want to see evidence of this achievement in the form of certification from the awarding body using the three-year rule. Evidence of achievement should be less than three years old. (Remember, this is a general guide only.)

What is the process for accrediting APA?

Information is obtained as follows:

- Pre-course questionnaires are sent to learners before they start their induction.

- Learners are asked to bring their completed questionnaire and copies of their certificates to induction.

- At the initial visit assessors will use the Introductory Form to discuss and record APA/APE/APL.

Who is involved in identifying APA/APE/APL?

The learner's employer

All employers from the workplace give feedback following the recruitment/ selection process.

Recycle Training

The trainer will collect the pre-course questionnaire from the learners at induction day. They will then consider the certificates presented and make a decision based on the following criteria:

- The qualifications and experience are relevant to the framework.

- The records/workplace activity/learning/qualifications are current, and the currency of dates on the certificate is checked using the qualification rule.

- The certificate is checked for authenticity and a photocopy is forwarded to the quality assurance administration team.

The trainer will record any credits on the accreditation form for APA/APE/APL provided.

This product evidence was used for these units:	The assessor also used these assessment methods:
L7 Prepare and develop resources to support learning L3 Identify individual learning aims and programmes	■ Professional discussion, to establish how resources can be developed and used ■ Observation of the candidate, using the guide with learners as part of agreeing their programmes

Myths about examination of products

Here are some myths that have grown up around examination of products and what assessors say about them:

Myth 1: Set them a project to cover the standards

'Projects and assignments are great for learning and development but you can't set one for assessment.'

Myth 2: You have to see the product evidence in the working context

'It's difficult to see plumbing behind the walls and underneath the floorboards.'

'In contract work, the plasterers' work gets painted over the minute it's dry.'

'When I go into the nursing home, this would mean seeing Mrs Jones toileted, bathed, dressed and fed at least three times.'

'When it's all been tarmac'd over by 4 o'clock you have to find other ways to check that the job was done to standard.'

6 Other methods

So far, this guide has looked at the most frequently used methods of assessing candidates. There are however, a number of other options you may need to use. This section contains help and guidance on some of these other activities and assessment methods that you may come across as an assessor. They are:

- *assessing prior learning, experience and achievement*

- *using simulation*

- *testing*

- *using projects and assignments.*

Some NVQs contain an external element of assessment, particularly where large amounts of knowledge are involved. You may find that there is a regulatory requirement for an externally imposed quality check on assessment decisions in cases where awarding bodies have made it a requirement of their quality assurance processes.

Candidates' knowledge is usually the focus of this independent check: testing and/or using a test or project are the specified assessment methods as a result of this requirement. (You will find details of how to carry out any independent assessment within the specific NVQ assessment strategy.)

Remember…

- Be guided by the needs of your candidate and the competence you are aiming to capture when choosing assessment methods.

- Never be tempted to do more than required, just to be sure you have 'enough'. Don't use the methods and activities in this section to pad out candidates' evidence.

Assessing prior learning, experience and achievement

It is important to take account of your candidates' existing competence before they start their NVQ programmes. If they can show they are already competent, they needn't undergo unnecessary training or evidence collection to achieve the standards. However, you still need to use the main methods of assessment when assessing evidence of your candidates' competence.

Assessing prior experience and learning is about recognising any existing experience and knowledge the candidate brings with them. This forms part of initial assessment and the assessment planning process. Assessment of prior achievement is about you, the assessor, recognising and validating the candidates' previous achievements using the main methods of assessment, providing they meet the standards. (You may decide it's quicker and more efficient to gather current evidence if your candidate works under similar conditions.)

The questions to ask when assessing prior learning, experience or achievement are set out in the table below.

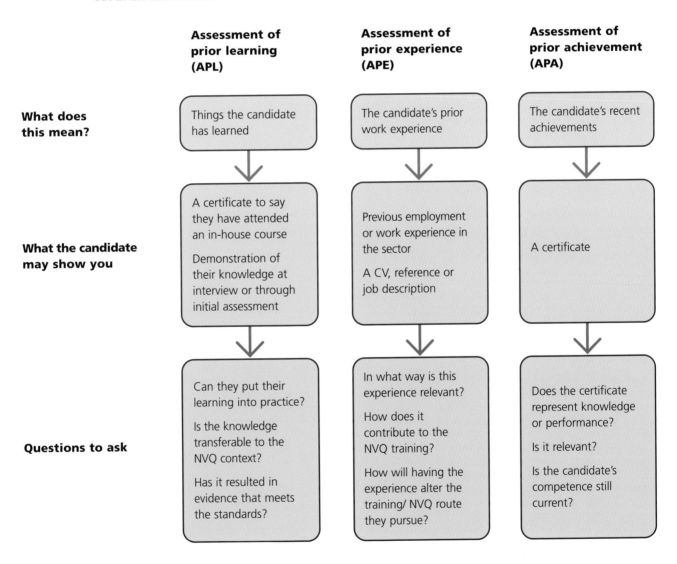

	Assessment of prior learning (APL)	Assessment of prior experience (APE)	Assessment of prior achievement (APA)
What does this mean?	Things the candidate has learned	The candidate's prior work experience	The candidate's recent achievements
What the candidate may show you	A certificate to say they have attended an in-house course Demonstration of their knowledge at interview or through initial assessment	Previous employment or work experience in the sector A CV, reference or job description	A certificate
Questions to ask	Can they put their learning into practice? Is the knowledge transferable to the NVQ context? Has it resulted in evidence that meets the standards?	In what way is this experience relevant? How does it contribute to the NVQ training? How will having the experience alter the training/ NVQ route they pursue?	Does the certificate represent knowledge or performance? Is it relevant? Is the candidate's competence still current?

Recording and providing an audit trail

Certificates and projects on their own do not constitute evidence of competence: you need to treat them as you would any other evidence using methods such as observation, professional discussion or asking for another's contribution – to confirm the content of a course or a CV for example. You then need to arrive at your assessment decision in the usual way, by asking:

Is the evidence:

- **V**alid?   Is it an appropriate way to judge competence in the learner's current context?

- **A**uthentic?   Has the evidence been produced by the learner?

- **C**urrent?   Does it show that the learner is still competent?

- **S**ufficient?   Is there enough evidence to meet the range of conditions and knowledge requirements of the standards?

'I use APL/APE within the NHS BT (Blood and Transplant), recognising their technical training programme by matching it against the health care standards. The programme logbook includes work-based assessments, training input, formal testing, witness testimony and candidate reports.'

Remember...

There is no formula for choosing the right assessment methods when you're dealing with evidence of APL/APE/APA, but a comprehensive professional discussion is often a good starting point.

Myths about APL/APE/APA

Here are some myths that have grown up around APL/APE/APA and what assessors say about them:

Myth 1: You can use certificates as evidence of competence because the candidate has already been assessed

> *'I had to tell one senior manager that the fellowship and the degree he had framed on his walls weren't proof of his managerial competence. He huffed and puffed and shouted at me. He thought he was in for a rubber-stamping exercise.'*

Myth 2: Evidence from APL/APE/APA has to be less than two years old

> *'One of my candidate training co-ordinators started her staff development strategy over two years ago. Am I going to tell her it's not current? Of course not!'*

Myth 3: Evidence from APL/APE/APA means less work for the assessor

> *'It seems to me that there are good reasons why evidence from APL/APE/APA is not widely used, attractive though it may seem initially. I have only used it with candidates where evidence in the current workplace is unavailable or scarce. The reason for this is simple: once we looked at the work involved in having to access paperwork and ensure currency and authenticity (sometimes the appropriate witness is no longer there) it is usually quicker and easier to obtain new evidence from the current workplace.'*

Using simulation

'When you're assessing first aid, you can't resuscitate a live person.'

Simulation isn't an assessment method: it's an environment that's as close to working conditions as possible and is only used when it's impossible for the candidate to perform in real life. It has to replicate the work environment and is usually used in situations where there are issues of cost, confidentiality, privacy, sensitivity or safety, or (as in the case above) it's unfeasible.

'I was observing my candidate deal with a "major incident" when one of the fatalities got up and went to the loo! Someone "forgot" their severed limb and left it in the middle of the road.'

'I make a point of asking the other "players" what they thought of the candidate's performance – how sensitively they felt they were treated, for example.'

Simulation can include the use of realistic work environments such as hairdressing salons or restaurants within colleges. However, you must comply with the strict regulations about these simulated environments set out in the NVQ assessment strategy or by your awarding body.

Simulation is not allowed within an increasing number of NVQs such as the Learning and Development Awards (including the A1 and V1 units for assessors and verifiers) and NVQs in Customer Care. This is because all the activities needed to demonstrate competence occur naturally for these qualifications, so there is no need for simulation.

Remember...

- Make sure you read your NVQ assessment strategy. This tells you if you can use simulation – an increasing number of NVQs do not allow it – and if so, when and how.

- Never use simulation as an easy way for candidates to demonstrate performance evidence that may not have occurred naturally within your chosen timescale. This is not a valid means of providing evidence.

Fire fighting

Here's an extract from the assessment strategy for fire fighting and some of the standards they relate to. You will see the reasons for using a simulated environment when you read the unit and element titles.

All approved centres have to meet the following principles:

Simulation must:

- include a comprehensive range of demands, activities and constraints relevant to those that would be met in a real working context

- provide individuals with access to the normal facilities, support and advice that would be available in the context and type of working situation

- ensure that formative assessment and advice are available from people with current experience of work being done

- realistically reflect normal working contexts and conditions

- place individuals under pressure of time, resources and demands that would operate in a normal working environment

- be used in accordance with guidelines at unit/element level in N/SVQs

- be planned, developed and documented by the centre in a way that ensures that simulations correctly reflect what the standard seeks to assess (validity).

In addition:

- a centre's overall strategy for simulation must be examined and approved by the awarding body's external verifier

- there should be a number of different simulations to cover the same aspect of standards in order to reduce the risk of collusion.

Units and elements

FF3: Save and preserve endangered life

FF3.1 Conduct a search to locate life involved in incidents

FF3.2 Rescue life involved in incidents

FF3.3 Provide treatment to casualties

FF3.4 Support people involved in rescue operations

FF4: Resolve operational incidents

FF4.1 Control and extinguish fires

FF4.2 Resolve incidents other than those involving a fire or hazardous materials

FF4.3 Support people involved in an operational incident

FF5: Protect the environment from the effects of hazardous materials

FF5.1 Mitigate damage to the environment from hazardous materials

FF5.2 Decontaminate people and property affected by hazardous materials

FF5.3 Support people involved in hazardous materials incidents

Making the most of simulation

Here are some suggestions from assessors:

'Successful simulations take a huge amount of planning and preparation. You need to allow time and resources, otherwise they aren't worth doing – you don't get the performance evidence you need.'

'Make sure you cover as much as possible in the way of standards. It's worth considering extending them to include unusual situations or special circumstances.'

'Remember that the product evidence the candidate produces is real, and you can assess it against the standards as normal.'

Recording and providing an audit trail

If you are assessing candidates within a simulated environment, you still use the main assessment methods just as you would when assessing under real working conditions. (Conditions may be simulated, but the assessment is real.)

Although you will be using observation during the simulation itself, you need to concentrate on the areas that differ significantly from reality, and address these using a combination of the main assessment methods. For example:

- observing your learner carrying out the simulated activity and then assessing any products that emerge from this

- using a witness testimony, particularly if the person in question has seen the candidate perform for real

- questioning the candidate before, during or immediately after the simulation: asking them how they would act, for example

- holding a professional discussion where the candidate brings along products to support their claim to competence.

You need to reach your assessment decision using VACS (see page 8), and record your decision as you would when carrying out any observation.

See section 7, Keeping it simple, page 67, for more about recording assessment decisions.

A myth about simulation

What's wrong with this? (The answer's at the bottom of the page if you don't know.)

'When we assess our machinists using the cutting machine we use plastic foam, not metal.'

Answer: NVQs are about performing under real-life working conditions, so unless the engineers use real materials as specified in the standards, they can't achieve them.

Testing

Some competence-based qualifications (such as key skills) contain an element of testing as part of the overall qualification requirements. There are NVQs, too (motor vehicle is an example), where passing a test is a mandatory part of the NVQ achievement. In these cases, you will be required to implement the testing as stipulated by the awarding body.

Preparing for tests

If your centre uses testing, you will need procedures in place for both preparing learners and managing the tests.

Preparing candidates

▪ Make sure that candidates are ready to be entered for the test (otherwise you are setting them up for failure).

▪ Help candidates acquire test techniques such as knowing how to deal with online or multi-choice questions.

▪ Allow them to practise under test conditions, using appropriate equipment and timing them.

Managing the tests

▪ Ensure the security of test papers: for example, you'll need procedures in place for receiving, storing and returning completed papers.

▪ Have procedures for dealing with candidates with particular requirements. One example might be to allow a supervised rest period to a candidate with a physical disability. Your awarding body will have guidelines.

▪ Have enough trained staff in place to administer and invigilate, and to be on hand in case of emergencies during the test.

▪ Communicate results and send certificates out to candidates. (There's often a delay between the test result and receiving the certificate so it's important not to lose touch with the candidate during this time.)

Using projects and assignments

Projects and assignments are sometimes used as a means of independently assessing learners, for example within accountancy and NVQs aimed at teaching assistants.

If you are planning to use projects or assignments within your centre, it's important to know why you're using them. Use the checklist below to help you decide.

Self-check: the purpose of projects and assignments

Answer the following questions and use the feedback below to help you establish your main purpose:

	Yes	No
1 Do you want to help the learner apply and develop the skills in which they will need to demonstrate competence?	☐	☐
2 Do you want to assess learners' ability and how they apply knowledge?	☐	☐
3 Do you want a cohort of learners to generate evidence for their portfolios?	☐	☐

If you have answered yes to 1, then projects and assignments can be a helpful way of achieving this. If, however, you have answered yes to 2 or 3, you need to consider the following:

Evidence of competence must be individual to each candidate. You can't give all your candidates the same project or assignment for them to demonstrate their individual knowledge and ability. Instead, projects should come from everyday, naturally occurring work activities. You should plan for this using a variety of assessment methods including observation, evidence from others, examination of products and professional discussion or questioning.

If you already do all of these, why do you need a project or assignment too?

A word about subcontractors...

If you use subcontractors and you know they are using projects and assignments with candidates, you may need to ask about the purpose of these, using the questions above. Be prepared to intervene if you think they are being used inappropriately.

Assessment for learning versus assessment of learning

With projects and assignments, you may find it useful to differentiate between assessment *for* learning and assessment *of* learning. The first is where learners acquire skills and knowledge and develop these through activities, feedback and practice at work. You 'assess' their progress, usually as part of the review process. (Projects and assignments may be among the activities used to develop their knowledge and skills.)

When you judge that they are performing competently to the standards, you can then carry out assessment *of* learning. This is where the learner demonstrates to you, the assessor, how they meet the standards by applying the knowledge and skills they have developed. In this context, projects and assignments are unlikely to be a valid way of assessing competence.

7 Keeping it simple

All those involved in the assessment of NVQs need to be able to trust that the assessor has reached the right decision about a candidate's competence. This means that you need to ensure that the process you used to arrive at your decision is transparent and open. Providing an audit trail for each assessment method, as described in other sections of this guide, is a vital part of assessing, as it creates a clear path for your internal and external verifiers to follow when they are sampling assessment within your centre.

This section will help you – and others involved in the verification process – to keep track of your assessment decisions and how you arrived at them, while keeping paperwork to a minimum.

Streamlining evidence

'I've seen V1 candidates bring in two lever arch files full of evidence. There's no need: you can see all the records in the filing cabinet when you go on an assessment visit.'

An overriding aspect of recording assessment decisions is knowing when to copy evidence and when to record where the evidence is located. Bear in mind that:

- candidates don't have to put all their evidence into a portfolio: instead, you can assess it *in situ* (the place where it's normally kept) and keep a record of the location as part of your assessment decision. (Learners can keep a record of what they've been doing as they learn. This is helpful when reviewing and establishing how much progress has been made, but you need to be clear about the difference between learning and competence.)

- your internal verifier (IV) will be sampling the assessment decision-making process to see if you've interpreted the standards correctly and in line with other assessors. If there's a dispute or the evidence isn't clear, your IV may ask to see it, so you need to keep a record of where it's kept as part of your assessment decision.

'For some awards – like those for Advice and Guidance – the external verifier wouldn't be allowed to look at evidence like client records in situ *because of confidentiality, so anonymous copies are included in the portfolio. I am all for minimalist portfolios, but we need to bear in mind the nature of the evidence and the requirements of the sector.'*

Streamlining assessment records

The NVQ Code of Practice requires that candidate assessment records give details of:

- who assessed what and when
- the assessment decision
- the assessment methods used for each unit/component
- the location of the supporting evidence.

The following tables show the evidence requirements for the A1 Assessors award.

The Assessor (AI) Award

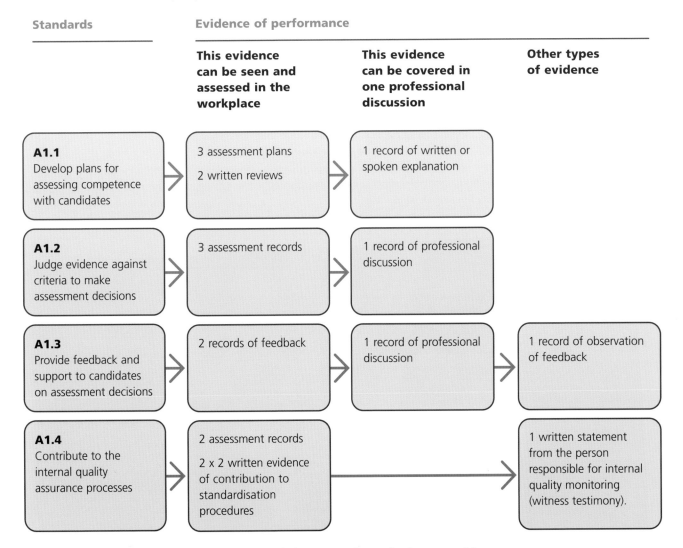

Standards	Evidence of performance		
	This evidence can be seen and assessed in the workplace	**This evidence can be covered in one professional discussion**	**Other types of evidence**
A1.1 Develop plans for assessing competence with candidates	3 assessment plans 2 written reviews	1 record of written or spoken explanation	
A1.2 Judge evidence against criteria to make assessment decisions	3 assessment records	1 record of professional discussion	
A1.3 Provide feedback and support to candidates on assessment decisions	2 records of feedback	1 record of professional discussion	1 record of observation of feedback
A1.4 Contribute to the internal quality assurance processes	2 assessment records 2 x 2 written evidence of contribution to standardisation procedures		1 written statement from the person responsible for internal quality monitoring (witness testimony).

The following evidence of knowledge required can also be covered in one professional discussion. All the evidence that can be covered during professional discussion may also be covered as a result of the observation process.

Evidence of knowledge

a A record of a professional discussion between the assessor and assessor-candidate during which the assessor reviews any method of the assessment not covered by performance evidence and:

i indicates the validity and reliability of each method

ii reviews any potential issues of fairness and access in relation to individual assessment methods

iii covers all the following methods if not covered by performance evidence:

- questioning
- APE and APA
- formal testing
- projects and assignments
- simulations
- candidate and peer reports
- witness testimony.

b A written or spoken explanation of the following procedures used within the assessor candidate's centre:

- how to provide access to assessment for candidates with individual special needs and special assessment requirements
- how disputes and appeals about assessment decisions are handled
- the internal standardisation and quality assurance arrangements
- how assessments are recorded
- sources of information regarding assessment requirements and best practice.

You can see from the evidence requirements that all that's needed for your A1 portfolio are the following items:

- a record of the assessment decisions along with details of the location of the other documentary (product) evidence

- a record of the observation of feedback (the portfolio is the best place for this)

- the written statement from the person responsible for internal quality assurance

- a tape containing a professional discussion.

Your own portfolio doesn't have to be exactly the same, but this gives you an idea of how you can keep paperwork to a minimum. It shows that it is possible to find ways to streamline evidence requirements and reduce the burden of evidence gathering on your candidates for the NVQs you assess. It is not good practice to work through the evidence requirements one by one.

Going online

'When I undertook the CIPD Online Learning Tutor course I completed a variety of activities online, both individually and collaboratively with other students. These were submitted to the tutor online for assessment and feedback as the course progressed. At the end of the course all my work was submitted in the form of an electronic portfolio for summative assessment.'

You can go online with candidates and get them to send you their evidence electronically if appropriate. Here, you're using the computer as a means of communication, not an assessment method in itself. (Don't confuse this with online testing where users answer questions online and get feedback concerning the correct answer and an overall score, mark or percentage.)

It is useful for candidates to transfer evidence electronically to the assessor for immediate feedback or support.

'I'm a care assessor and all my candidates work shifts. I get them to send me their evidence electronically whenever they like – it's invaluable.'

'We have learners in call centres all over the country. They talk to their assessor online using the company intranet. We're set up for it and it's good use of time.'

Giving feedback online

When going online, remember to use the principles of giving effective feedback:

1 **Start with the positive.** What has the candidate done well? For example: 'Your observation report was very clear. You used a narrative approach that was easy to follow.'

2 **Say what didn't go so well.** For example: 'You didn't explain why you awarded the candidate assessor the standards in question. You need to explain your decision.'

3 **Be specific** about what needs to happen next, such as: 'You need to write a short paragraph explaining how you arrived at your assessment decision. Do this by explaining how what the candidate did met the standards in question'.

4 **Keep to the point** and write in short, clear sentences. This is especially important for written feedback (via email or similar). Use bullets or numbered lists if you have a number of points to make, or for action points, particularly if you want the candidate to do more than one or two things as a result of your feedback.

5 **Use 'you'** when writing your online feedback. Avoid the passive voice ('it was noted …') as this can sound overly formal.

About ENTO

ENTO is an independent, self-financing knowledge organisation, experienced in national vocational standards and qualifications development and the provision of support products and services.

Since 1988, ENTO has built an unparalleled track record and capability in the development of national occupational standards and national vocational qualifications (NVQs). Our work helps people develop their level of competency and skills, and is focused on the needs of learners, employees and employers. We also have responsibility for the promotion and monitoring of the matrix standard, a quality standard for any organisation that gives information, advice and guidance.

ENTO is unique in that it represents, across all sectors, those whose occupation requires them to deal with people in the workplace: information, advice and guidance people; learning and development trainers; personnel people; recruitment consultants; trade union and learning representatives; and health and safety at work practitioners.

Because of this role, people for whom ENTO standards and qualifications have been developed, have a significant influence on the take-up of vocational qualifications throughout the workplace and at all levels. ENTO currently maintains 9 suites of National Occupational Standards covering 11 occupational areas, 23 NVQs, 4 Apprenticeships and 3 suites of non-qualification based standards.

The Learning Network for assessors and verifiers

The Learning Network is a members-only website used by assessors and verifiers across all sectors and disciplines. The network's main aim is to enhance the continuous professional development of assessors and verifiers by equipping them with up-to-date information, providing a forum for discussion and sharing of best practice and the opportunity to influence what is happening in the whole assessment and verification arena.

If you would like to join the Learning Network or find out more, please contact:

Sarah Williams
Sales & Marketing Coordinator

Tel: 02920 436666
Email: sarahwilliams@ento.co.uk

Alternatively, you can visit www.thelearningnetworkonline.com